THE CHEAPSKATE'S HANDBOOK

THE
CHEAPSKATE'S
HANDBOOK

A Guide to the Subtleties, Intricacies and Pleasures
of Being a Tightwad

by

MIFFLIN LOWE

PRICE/STERN/SLOAN
Publishers, Inc., Los Angeles
1986

a dmc book
published by
Price/Stern/Sloan Publishers, Inc.
410 North La Cienega Boulevard
Los Angeles, California 90048

Printed in the United States of America
ISBN: 0-8431-1246-8

CONTENTS

INTRODUCTION: CHEAPSKATES, COME OUT OF THE CLOSET!

To date, no one has asked me why I've written this book. I believe this is for a very good reason – **NO ONE WANTS TO ADMIT THEY'RE CHEAP!** To be branded cheap is to be the worst sort of pariah! Even the word "cheapskate" seems to make the chin tremble as it perches on the lips.

To me, this is amazing.

In a society in which people of every conceivable psychological and sexual stripe are ready to step forth on the Donahue Show and blandly assert that they're kitten whippers, dog stranglers, shoe sniffers – almost anything at all – not one person has yet had the courage to come forth and say simply, "Yes, I'm a cheapskate. "

Well, I say it's time to stop trembling and denying! I say it's time to stop cringing and dissimulating! It's time to stand up and be counted (and make sure you get the right change)! It's time to say it loud, "I'm cheap and I'm proud!"

There, doesn't that feel better? Doesn't it feel great?

As for *The Cheapskate's Handbook,* please – take it, read it, enjoy it and learn from it.

And above all, pay for it.

Sincerely,

Mifflin Lowe

Mifflin Lowe

1

MISERLINESS APTITUDE TEST

Are you a spendthrift or a cheapskate? Take this test and see how you rate.

1. **If you drop a popsicle in the dirt, you will:**
   (a) leave it there   (b) try to give it to a dog
   (c) wash it off and eat it.

2. **What sobers you up faster?**
   (a) a cup of black coffee   (b) the thought of overtipping?

3. **How short will you let a pencil get before you consider using a new one?**
   (a) 5 inches   (b) 3 inches   (c) less than an inch.

4. **Have you ever seriously considered leaving a restaurant without paying the bill?**
   Yes   No

5. **Have you ever written anyone out of your will?**
   Yes   No

6. **Do you automatically check for forgotten change in a pay telephone?**
   Yes   No

7. **Have you ever considered stealing toilet paper from a public restroom?**
   Yes   No

Would you eat this or give it to a dog?

8. Have you ever coasted down a hill in your car to save gas even though you weren't in danger of running out?
    Yes   No

9. Do you automatically count your change when leaving a check-out counter?
    Yes   No

10. If you went into a market and saw a bin filled with free sample packages of a new detergent, how many would you take?
    (a) One   (b) two or three   (c) as many as you could carry.

11. If you were draining three pieces of bacon, how many paper towels would you use?
    (a) two   (b) one   (c) one-half

12. If you get a letter on which the stamp is not clearly cancelled, will you consider steaming it off and reusing it?
    Yes   No

13. How far would you drive a "guest" passenger before you would consider asking him to split the gas?
    (a) 200 miles or more   (b) 100 miles   (c) around the block.

14. What was your reaction when you opened your first joint checking account?
    (a) none   (b) cried all night   (c) took an almost lethal dose of aspirin.

15. If someone were handing out free promotional packages of cigarettes, would you take one even though you don't smoke?
    Yes   No

16. **Do you unwrap Christmas and birthday gifts carefully so you can save the ribbon and paper?**
Yes   No

17. **How old does an article of clothing have to be before you'd consider giving it to the Salvation Army?**
(a) one year or less   (b) two to four years
(c) three generations.

18. **How far out of your way will you walk to pick up a dime?**
(a) 0-3 feet   (b) 3-6 feet   (c) ¼ mile.

19. **Have you ever washed a piece of previously used Saran Wrap and reused it?**
Yes   No

20. **What do you do with pencils you get from a miniature golf course?**
(a) throw them away   (b) put them in a pocket and forget about them   (c) collect them for resale.

21. **If someone offers to take you out for lunch, will you go even if you've just eaten?**
Yes   No

22. **How can you tell when it's too cold in your house?**
(a) when the temperature falls beneath 65 degrees
(b) when ice forms on the inside of windows
(c) when someone drops dead.

23. **To you, the most depressing thing about Christmas is:**
(a) the crass commercialism
(b) the exploitation of a sacred occasion
(c) knowing that prices will go down December 26th.

24. **Your idea of having a really good party is:**
(a) a surprise party   (b) a come-as-you-are party   (c) a BYOB party.

25. **If you went to a restaurant that served all the lobster you could eat for $20, how would you know when you were finished?**
(a) when you'd had one or two lobsters and felt satisfied
(b) when you'd thrown up
(c) when your stomach needed pumping.

26. **How far under a refrigerator will you reach to recover a penny?**
(a) three to five inches   (b) one to two feet
(c) the entire length of your arm.

27. **How long will you use a disposable razor?**
(a) two times   (b) two weeks   (c) two years.

28. **If you squeeze too much toothpaste on your brush, will you try to get some of it back in the tube?**
(a) yes   (b) no   (c) maybe

29. **When you go to a restaurant will you ask for extra tartar sauce even if you don't order anything you could possibly use it on — just because it's free?**
(a) Yes   (b) No   (c) not tartar sauce, but ketchup maybe.

How to Score

Give yourself 5 points for every "yes" answer, 7 points for every "c" answer, and 10 points if you answered "b" on questions 1 or 25. Award yourself a 15 point bonus if you have already written someone out of your will (see question 5).

Rating

0-10	A real wastrel, no miser potential
10-20	Prodigal son
20-30	Scattergood and squanderer
30-40	Spendthrift
40-50	Idle and extravagant
50-60	Penny wise but pound foolish
60-70	Approaching minginess
70-80	Thrifty
80-90	Frugal
90-100	Potential pinchpenny
100-110	True tightwad
110-120	Undeniable cheapskate
120-130	Approaching stinginess
130-140	Unquestionably niggardly
140-150	Genuine skinflint
150-160	A regular muckworm
160 and over	MISER

If you scored 155 or more, READ NO FURTHER! You're already cheaper than most people, and that's just plain astonishing. If you scored less than 150, read on. You've still got a lot to learn.

2

Tips On Tipping

There's nothing more painful than tipping someone who's going to give you lousy service and is probably getting paid a lot more than he/she should anyway. The following is a handy but by no means complete list of infractions which will allow you to reduce the amount you leave as a tip with complete justification. Take the charts with you whenever you go to a restaurant, get into a cab, or leave on a business trip.

Waiters/Waitresses

Unless a waiter or waitress actually loses an arm or leg while serving you, there's no reason to tip them 15%, let alone, God forbid, 20%. Here are a few ways you can cut the tip down to size.

Infraction	Subtraction
Slow service	− 7 to 12%
Surly behavior	Automatic 15% penalty
Bad vibes	− 2%
Bad food	− 3%
Bad breath	− 14%
Crumbs from previous dinner left on table	− 9%
Cold food (should be hot)	− 4%
Hot food (should be cold)	− 4%
Too talkative	Up to 8%
Not talkative enough	Up to 8%

Plastic bugs, available at any joke shop, will not only
help you avoid paying a tip but also the bill.

Condescending	Up to 10%
Error on check (your favor)	No penalty
Error on check (*not* in your favor)	Automatic 15% penalty
Waiter doesn't laugh at your joke	Automatic 15% penalty

$CHEAP TRICK #1: If you're dining with other people, always underestimate the amount of tip you owe. Someone will always make up the difference.

$CHEAP TRICK #2: Always grumble and complain throughout the entire meal, thus preparing the waiter for the reduced tip he will receive.

$CHEAP TRICK #3: *Never* tip on the tax.

Cab Drivers

It's difficult to imagine why taxi drivers think the world owes them a 20% tip on top of the outrageous fares they charge. Careful observation and application of the following rules will usually cut a cabbie's tip down to a more reasonable percentage – like nothing.

Infraction	Subtraction
Drives too fast	– 10%
Doesn't drive fast enough	– 10%
Swerves too much	– 10%
Tells you about his children	– 15%
Uses four letter word more than 12 times in one sentence	– 3%

Spits out window (window open)	− 6%
Spits out window (window closed)	− 12%
Doesn't open the door for you	− 20%
Uses horn more than 150 times in one mile	− 2%
Failure to laugh at your joke	Automatic 20% penalty

Doormen

There's almost nothing in the world more infuriating than having to pay someone to open a door you could have easily opened yourself. The following are acceptable reasons for walking past a doorman without leaving a tip.

Infraction	Subtraction
Door not open wide enough	No tip
Door open too wide	No tip
Stain on trousers	No tip
Fringe on epaulets out of place	No tip
Socks don't match	No tip
Looks like Cesar Romero	No tip
Failure to laugh at your joke	No tip

$CHEAP TRICK #4: Remember, you *never* have to tip the owner of a barber shop or beauty salon. When you make an appointment at one of these places, always make sure it's with the person who owns the place.

3

How To Live With A Roommate

Remember, a roommate is nothing but a predator in disguise.

1. Keep everything you possibly can in your room.
2. Put your name on anything you can't keep in your room.
3. If you buy sliced baloney, bread or cheese, count the number of slices.
4. Whenever possible, use your roommate's shampoo, shaving cream or laundry detergent.
5. Buy your own toilet paper and keep it in your room. Take only as much as you'll need on each trip to the bathroom.
6. If you buy a bottle of milk, liquor, floor wax, mouthwash or cologne, mark it to show how much you've used. If your roommate uses any, charge him.
7. Don't let your roommate watch your television. Say it wears out the tubes.
8. Whenever possible, eat your roommate's cereal, Pop Tarts or canned peanuts.
9. Never lend your roommate a stamp.
10. Never lend your roommate more than a dime.
11. Make sure your roommate's name – and not yours – goes on the lease, phone bill and all utility contracts.

On any trip to the bathroom, take only as much toilet
paper as you'll need.

Here's a list of charges you may reasonably expect to assess a roommate when he/she uses anything of yours. Snip and attach to the refrigerator door for convenient reference.

Roommate Fee List

Item	Fee
Stereo record	1 play/5¢ 3 plays/12¢ Album/25¢
Hair dryer	15¢ per minute up to 3 minutes, 4¢ each additional minute
Toilet tissue	3¢ per sheet × _____ sheet
Cereal	Corn Flakes/12¢ bowl Shredded Wheat/4¢ bowl Sugar Smacks/$1.10 bowl
Cue Tip	4¢ each
Band Aid	7¢ each
Socks, underwear, bra, panties, pantyhose	Clean/75¢ per day Previously worn/36¢ per day

Leftover turkey sandwich	75¢
Eggroll	25¢
Sheets	Clean/$1 per night Previously used/35¢ per night

4

How To Make The Most Of Your Neighbors

Remember, God put people next door to you for one main reason: so you can borrow things. In fact, with proper cultivation there are many things and services you can reasonably expect to get from your neighbors free of charge for the rest of your life.

Things you should expect to borrow from your neighbors (suburban).

1. Weedeater
2. Lawn chairs
3. Tree pruning tool
4. Ant traps
5. 12 lbs. of charcoal, 1½ quarts of lighter fluid
6. Prince tennis racket
7. Plumber's helper
8. Ice cream making machine

Things you should expect to borrow from your neighbors (urban).

1. Roach motel
2. Roach clip
3. .38 caliber handgun
4. Gold lamé pants
5. Plumber's helper
6. Disposable syringe

$CHEAP TRICK$ #'s 5, 6, 7:

5) Always treat your neighbors like gold – smile and say hello whenever you see them. Make complimentary remarks about their children and encourage them to borrow an egg, a stick of margarine, a cup of sugar or anything that costs less than $1.50. This will make it a lot easier when you ask to move into their vacation home for a week.

6) Once you borrow something from a neighbor, there's nothing that says you have to give it back – until they ask for it.

7) Don't forget to ask your neighbors if you can have the newspaper after they're done with it.

5

AFTER ALL, WHAT ARE FRIENDS FOR?

J ust as there are different grades of meat, so are there different classes of friends. So, just like your mother said, choose your friends carefully.

GROUP 1 – PERSONAL FRIENDS
These are the people who can get you free tickets, help you on moving day and will baby-sit for nothing. These are also the people who are most likely to hit you up for a loan. If you ever have to choose between friends, these are the first to go.

1.   Ushers at a movie theater.
2.   Anyone who'll take care of your dog while you're away.
3.   Anyone who'll give you a ride to the airport.
4.   Anyone who'll let you shop at the PX with his/her card.
5.   Podiatrists.

GROUP 2 – CLOSE, PERSONAL FRIENDS
These are people who can get you something at dealer cost or can give you free advice that might otherwise cost $50 an hour. You might occasionally consider inviting them over for dinner.
1.   Appliance dealers and clothing wholesalers.
2.   Anyone who can get you a discount on airline tickets.
3.   Lawyers and smart stock brokers.

4. Someone who owns a tuxedo that's your size (male).
5. Someone who wears the same size shoe (female).
6. Dentists, optometrists, otorhinolaryngologists.

GROUP 3 — VERY GOOD, CLOSE, PERSONAL FRIENDS

These are people who deserve all the respect, love and attention you can shower on them, for they can save you an easy $1,500 a year. Consider inviting them over for dinner once a week.

1. Anyone who owns a pool, boat or vacation home.
2. Anyone who lives near a ski slope.
3. Tax assessors and IRS auditors.
4. Jewelers, furriers and new car dealers.
5. Heart specialists, oncologists, urologists.

$CHEAP TRICK #8: Never be the first to buy anything that's new on the market. Let a friend get it first and see if it's worth it.

FUNDAMENTAL PRINCIPLE
A friend in need is someone you don't need to know.

6

How To Get Invited To A Friend's Summer House

If a friend has a pool, boat, or home in a vacation area, you should be able to use it at least three weekends a year. Remember, however, that nobody is going to just invite you to a summer house, you have to work for it. Follow this plan and you'll wind up spending summer weekends at a friend's place and not at some expensive motel.

1. Send a Christmas card. Don't send one that includes a picture of the wife and kids, however. You don't want to remind him of how many people are in your family.

2. Send a birthday gift. Something they can use in the pool, at the beach, or on the boat.

3. In late May, take your friend out for a couple of drinks. While you're at it, tell him that your 18-year-old daughter has just bought a bikini that's *absolutely scandalous*. Or that your wife is working out at a health spa and looks great.

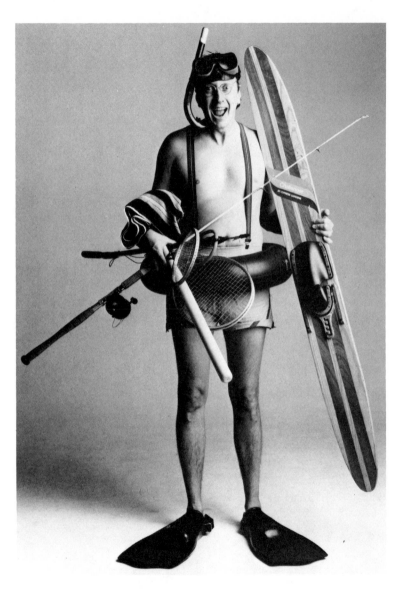

The "Hi, we're here" approach is rarely effective and almost never includes a meal.

7
How To Go On A Ski Weekend With Friends

1. Borrow all the equipment you'll need. Rentals are expensive.

2. Drive up in someone else's car. Pay for half the gas on the way up and forget about it on the way home.

3. Pretend you're asleep every time the car approaches a toll booth.

4. Things you should refuse to pay for: toilet paper, vacuum cleaner bags, napkins, room deodorizers, dish powder, soap. If anyone asks, say you don't use them.

5. If you miss a meal, subtract 10% from your share of the weekend food bill; 2 meals, 20% and so on.

8

Cheap Eats – How To Go Out To Dinner With Friends

1. Always go to the restaurant in their car, so they pay for the gas, parking and tolls.
2. Hold the door and let them go in the restaurant first. If it's necessary to tip the maitre d' they'll have to do it.
3. Take your coat with you to the table or leave it in the car. Coat check people always will expect tips.
4. Try to get a table near the kitchen so you can complain about it all through the meal. It's the perfect excuse for cutting down on the tip.
5. Make as many mutual purchases as possible. Order a carafe of wine, a pitcher of beer, a platter of nachos, or whatever. Then drink and eat as much as you can as fast as you can.
6. Order the most expensive thing on the menu. If you end up splitting the tab, the other couple will be financing part of your meal.
7. Stuff yourself. And we're not just talking about food. We're talking about paper napkins, rolls and butter, salt and pepper, packets of mustard, ketchup and tartar sauce. After the meal, take as many toothpicks and mints as you can get in your pockets.

8.   Ask for a doggie bag. If your friends leave any food, make sure you get that, too.

$CHEAP TRICK #8: If you order pizza, count the number of slices and make sure you get at least your fair share. If there's an odd slice, eat fast so you'll get it.

$CHEAP TRICK #9: On occasions when you have to buy a meal for someone else (your parents, say, on their golden anniversary), let them order first, then tell them you intend to pick up the tab. If they know you're going to pay for the meal beforehand, they'll probably get something expensive. If they're not sure, they'll usually order something cheap.

CHEAP EATS – HOW TO RECOGNIZE A GOOD RESTAURANT

By good, of course, we mean cheap. Here are a few sure ways to recognize a place that's not going to charge you an arm and a leg for a leg of lamb.

1.   A neon sign with more than four letters that don't work.
2.   Cocktail napkins with jokes on them.
3.   Paper placemats – particularly ones with a map of the state or an ad for a local bowling alley.
4.   Waitresses who look like they sleep with bears.
5.   A chef who looks like a bear.
6.   A Shell No Pest strip hanging in the dining area.
7.   An owner who sits at the bar and picks his teeth.
8.   A "no tipping" sign.

9

No-No's: Things A Cheap Person Should Never Do

1. Buy ice cubes.

2. Pay for parking – when you can find a spot in an alley six blocks away.

3. Pay for a pay toilet – not when you can crawl under the door.

4. Order a soft drink with ice.

5. Go any place that has a cover charge.

6. Rent a golf cart – when you can convince your friends that *they* need exercise.

7. Accept a collect call.

10

Cheap Sentiment: The Fine Art Of Gift Giving

Remember, when you're giving something away, it isn't the thought that counts.

Whenever possible, give something homemade

Remember when you were a kid and gave your parents potholders, painted shells and crumby clay ashtrays? Remember how thrilled they were to get something just because you made it? Remember how thrilled you were to give it – because it didn't cost you a dime? Well, the same principle applies now. Not only are homemade gifts the cheapest things you can give, but people are reluctant to criticize them for fear of hurting your feelings. And don't worry if you can't paint, weave, knit or whatever; when it comes to homemade gifts, discernable talent is neither expected nor necessary.

Suggested List of Homemade Gifts

Imitation leather wallet	Neckerchief slide
Scarf	Knitted mittens
Macrame plant hanger	Guava jelly
Paint by number picture	Driftwood sculpture
Shell ashtray	Feather underpants

Give something religious

If the recipient of the gift is a member of an organized religion, you may give him an inexpensive medallion, painting, sacre coeur or book in the complete confidence that, no matter how cheap the gift is, no one will have the guts to point it out.

Sentimental favorites

If you don't want to make something homemade or give something religious, a great way to get off cheaply is to give a photo. For instance, take a picture of your brother's family on a summer picnic, then blow it up and give it at Christmas. For less than six bucks you're off the hook.

Search the attic, scour the basement

Look through the junk that's piling up in the far reaches of your house. You'd be surprised how many times you can come up with something that just needs to be dusted off or given some paint to make it look like a thoughtful gift.

Free samples, government publications

Samples of perfume, soap and cologne are available free in most department stores. Also, government publications such as *Dog Care, Raising Your Own Vegetables,* and *How to Care for a Snake Bite* are available at any U.S. Post Office.

$CHEAP TRICK #10: If you've bought someone a gift but you're not sure they got one for you, leave your gift in the car. If they give you something, you can always run out to the car and get your gift. Otherwise, forget it.

If you can't give something homemade, look for a suitable gift in the attic, cellar or garage.

$CHEAP TRICK #11: The most fundamental rule in gift exchanging is that of "parity." In simple terms, this means *never give anyone a gift that costs more than the last gift they gave you.* Keep a list.

$CHEAP TRICK #12: Remember, sentimentality costs you nothing, so really pour it on. Hugs, kisses, fond remembrances, short speeches, wistful tears and other effusions are invaluable in concealing the fact that your gift is worth a grant total of $1.98. In general, when actually handing over the gift, try to act as though you are giving up your only child to a gypsy slaver.

FUNDAMENTAL PRINCIPLE
Never buy anything new if you can get it used.

11

MOOCHING: THE SWEET SCIENCE

With the least bit of effort, there are some things you should never have to buy in your life, including cigarettes, french fries, gum, throat lozenges, stamps, paper clips, and fabric softener. There is, however, an *exact method* to mooching that must be followed if you expect to do it successfully.

Step 1: The Search

The most important part of the mooching process, it sets the foundation for everything that will follow. Thus it is critical that you make a credible and thorough search of your person and environs *as though you really expect to find the object you're about to mooch.*

Step 2: The Expression of Perplexion

At the end of your "search" pause reflectively and scratch your head. Say something like, "Gee, I was sure I had a fresh pack of gum with me."

Step 3: The Humble Request

The facial expression and body language should reek of humility, modesty and regret. Always make sure you apologize as you mooch. For instance, "Geez, I can't find my gum . . . d'ya mind if I bum a piece?"

Step 4: Thanks

Always thank your victim. It doesn't have to be effusive. Frequently, in fact, a wink and a nod will be more effective than a gushing thank you.

Step 5: The Promise

Always tell your victim you'll replace the item you've just mooched. Try not to laugh.

FUNDAMENTAL PRINCIPLE

Never buy when you can rent; never rent when you can mooch.

12

How To Fight Generous Impulses

You can't help it. Even with the best intentions, you're going to feel an occasional impulse to pay more than your share for a meal or give a friend a gift that's more expensive than the last one he gave you. You should not be shocked or embarassed by these feelings. They are perfectly natural and understandable. The following techniques will help you conquer these strange and discomforting feelings.

Think of all the people who are much richer than you'll ever be.

Think of the Rockefellers, the Gettys, the oil sheiks. Maybe they can afford to give money away, but you can't!

Remember the last time you got gypped.

How about the time you paid a quarter more than you really owed for lunch? How 'bout the time you got to a toll bridge and you were the only one with change? Keep such things in mind and you won't be so quick to give some snivelling Cub Scout fifty cents for UNICEF.

Remember that if the person you're being generous to had the same choice, he or she wouldn't be generous to you.

Ask yourself, "What am I going to get out of this?"

Answer yourself, "Probably a big fat nothing."

13

SHOPPING: THE BASICS

1. **Remember that a salesperson is your social inferior.** At most of our "better stores" salespeople generally act as though they're related to royalty. The reason is simple: by acting snobbish they think they can embarass a customer into making a purchase. Just remember, that even though a salesperson may act as though they're related to the Duke of Kent, they're probably going to take a bus home and have a bowl of canned soup for dinner.

2. **Remember, you can always get it cheaper.** It's all right to go to an expensive store and look for what you want, but once you've found it, head for a discount place. In fact, if you spend long enough looking for the best price, you can frequently avoid purchasing an item altogether. (See "How to Postpone a Purchase.")

3. **Never buy a status symbol.** It's one of a cheap person's greatest virtues that he is rarely impressed with the shallow pretensions of acquiring and displaying status symbols. This has a lot to do with the fact that status symbols cost about five times as much as cheap brands. In general, always try to buy a "generic" brand and *never* purchase anything that's been advertised in *Town and Country* magazine.

14

HAGGLING: HOW TO DO IT

One of the outstanding deficiencies in the American character is an inability to argue with a merchant about the price of anything. Other nations mock us for this. Look at the Turks, the Italians, the French. Do you, for one second, think they'd ever walk into a store, pay the full price and be able to leave with any sense of self respect? Whether they're buying a tomato, a car or an oriental rug, they argue, demean, rant and rave and finally get the price down. It's called *haggling*, and here's how to do it.

1. Feign disinterest.
2. Express contempt for the merchandise.
3. Offer one-third of its marked value.
4. Laugh at the merchant's reply.
5. Repeat your offer and stand firm.
6. If the merchant does not meet your price, walk to the door.
7. Make a final offer.
8. Leave.

When a merchant tells you the price of an article,
always laugh in disbelief.

15

How To Postpone A Purchase

S ay it's the beginning of summer and your wife is after you to buy a lawnmower. For the first two weeks, pretend to keep forgetting you ever discussed the subject. For the next two weeks, say you're going around to different stores, pricing lawnmowers. For the next two weeks, tell her it's right up there at the top of your list of things to do – by then it's late mid-summer, and you can tell her you're waiting for the end of season sales when you'll really get a good deal. At the end of the season, tell her there's no point in buying a lawnmower since you won't need it 'til next spring. Next spring, borrow your neighbor's lawnmower until the beginning of summer. Repeat process.

$CHEAP TRICK #13:
If you can't find what you want at the Salvation Army, go to a store that sells used merchandise or "seconds"; if you can't get it there, go to a discount store; if you can't get it at a discount store, forget it.

FUNDAMENTAL PRINCIPLE
Never buy anything at a place that spells shop as "shoppe."

16

How To Go Food Shopping

1. Take all the coupons you can.

2. Eat as much as you can while walking through the store to make sure the stuff is okay. Remember, you only pay for the grapes they weigh.

3. Eat as many free samples as you can. If they have a display with free donuts, don't be embarassed to eat them all.

4. Eliminate any non-edible part of any fruit you buy. Twist the tops off bananas, knock the nubs off mushrooms, rip off the stems on a bunch of grapes.

5. Read as many magazines and newspapers as you can while you're standing in the check-out line. Don't buy any of them.

6. Buy as many generic products as you can. Thirty minutes after the meal is over, no one will care whether they ate expensive peas or cheap ones.

7. Buy in quantity. By the age of twenty-three, a really smart shopper should have enough reduced price toilet paper to last the average family of five a lifetime.

By the time you reach the checkout counter, you should have already eaten the equivalent of a large lunch.

17
FACE FACTS

We strongly recommend that you learn how to tell the denomination of a coin – while it's still in your pocket – merely by feeling it with your fingertips. This is invaluable when you're forced to make a charitable contribution in public or when you're approaching a toll booth with other people in the car and the driver asks for change. Keep in mind that Jefferson's nose is larger than Roosevelt's but smaller than Washington's. Lincoln has the largest schnoz of all. Bless him.

18
Cheap Dates

Bear in mind that the only truly cheap date is the one you pick off a tree. However, it is possible to go on a date and keep expenses to a minimum. The most important thing is choosing the right person.

DATE SELECTION – HOW TO SPOT THE RIGHT WOMAN

1. Never date anyone your mother would characterize as a "floozy." Remember, cheap women are never cheap dates.
2. Never date anyone who wears that latest fashions. Buying expensive, new clothes is a sickness that can't be cured.
3. Never date anyone who points out a fur coat to you during casual conversation.
4. Never date anyone who looks at an expensive car and moans.
5. Never date anyone who mentions Acapulco, Cancun or Aruba.
6. Never date anyone who likes to window shop. Sooner or later, she'll want to start shopping for real.
7. Never date anyone with heels more than 2½″ high. She'll never be happy with what she's got. She'll always want something better, faster or higher priced.

DATE SELECTION – HOW TO SPOT THE RIGHT MAN

1. Never date anyone your mother would call a "character." Before the evening's over, he'll try to borrow your life savings.
2. Never date anyone who says he loves home cooking. What he really means is that he'd like to eat at your place – for free.
3. Never date anyone who says his idea of a "great time" is to stay at home and watch TV. He's only saying this because he knows it won't cost anything.
4. Never date anyone you meet at a fire sale. He'll never take you to a good restaurant and, if he does, he'll still smell like a charcoal briquet.
5. Never date anyone who wants to know what your father does for a living.
6. Never date anyone who wants to be a doctor. Before you know it, you'll be working and he'll be going to medical school.
7. Never date anyone who wears 2″ heels or elevator shoes. He'll never be happy with what he's got. He'll always want something better, faster or higher priced.

Places to Avoid
1. Restaurants with valet parking
2. Any bar that doesn't have jokes on its napkins
3. Any place with a doorman

Places to Go
1. An art museum (check for free hours)
2. A bookstore (browsing only)
3. Folk dancing performance at the YWCA
4. A library

5. A planetarium (check for free hours)
6. Any bar that has napkins with jokes on them
7. Reduced price movie matinees

Cheap Thrills: Things to Do that Won't Cost a Dime

1. **Comparison shopping** – See who can come up with the best price for pizza, rubber shoes or a pound of spaghetti.
2. **Clip coupons** – For variety, you might also consider cutting off box tops or collecting "proof of purchase" labels for refunds.
3. **Search for forgotten coins in pay phones.**
4. **Go to the beach with a metal detector** – If you've ever pulled a quarter out of the sand, you know the meaning of excitement.
5. **Look for money under the back seat of a car** – A great prelude to romance.
6. **Find returnable cans and bottles** – Just 'cause you did it as a kid isn't any reason you can't enjoy it now!
7. **Make things with Hamburger Helper** – It doesn't have to be a meal either. Make a chair, a sofa, even a lamp! When you start with Hamburger Helper the sky's the limit.
8. **Look through a porthole at a construction site** – Hours upon hours of lively entertainment.
9. **Look for change that's been dropped at the drive-in teller window of a bank.**

How To Take A Date Out To Dinner . . . If You Must

1. When the waiter asks if you want a drink, quickly say, "Just water" before your date has a chance to order some expensive fruity cocktail with a little umbrella in it.

The willingness to dutch-date is one of the surest signs
of true love and affection.

2. As soon as you get the menu, locate the four most expensive items. Talk about how bad they are. For example, "A friend once got botulism from the Beef Wellington. . . ."

3. Locate the two cheapest dishes on the menu. Tell your date they're the specialties of the house.

4. Never get coffee or dessert unless they come with the meal.

5. Ask for a doggie bag.

FUNDAMENTAL PRINCIPLE
A dutch date is better than a french kiss.

19

Cheap Mates
For Richer Or Poorer:
A Few Thoughts On
Marriage

When a cheap person marries, it is almost invariably for life. This is due in no small measure to the enormous costs of alimony, child support and continuing legal advice. This is not to say there aren't some good reasons to tie the knot. For one thing, if you marry right, you've got yourself a virtually inexhaustible source of free labor. For another, you'll never have to pay for a date again. Keep in mind, however, that there's a good reason they call it a "marriage contract" and that it's your money they're talking about. In truth, a genuinely cheap person will hardly ever marry. If you decide to, however, here are a few things you should look for during your search for the ideal mate.

1. **A LARGE NOSE.** A truly cheap person would not even consider spending money on something as frivolous as a nose job. A rough formula is this: the more your prospective spouse has spent making his/her nose small, the more that marriage will cost you.

2. **OLD CLOTHES.** 3-5 years old is good and the mousier the better. Hand-me-downs from Mom or Dad are ideal.

The ideal mate will not have a nose job.

3. **A ROTTEN HAIRCUT.** Look for a hairdo that looks like it was done with a hacksaw. Basically, the same rule applies here as with the nose job.

Finally, always look for someone who is able to say, "Sorry, my spouse already gave at the office" with a perfectly straight face. This, in fact, may be the single best criterion for selecting a mate. Before any promises are made, make sure your intended does it well.

Good Reasons to Marry a Cheap Man.

Sooner or later any woman is going to wonder why she should stay married to anyone as cheap as you. Invite her to consider the following.

1. Cheap men don't go to strip shows or porno palaces. Or anyplace else that has a $4 cover charge.
2. Cheap men don't go to bars. Not at $2.50 a drink!
3. Cheap men don't smoke. Not at $1.25 a pack!
4. Cheap men don't gamble. If they lose more than $1.50 they just head home in tears.
5. Cheap men are courageous. It takes guts to ask someone to split the gas after a ride around the block.
6. Cheap men are handy around the house. It's inconceivable that a cheap man would pay to have anyone do anything he could do himself.
7. Cheap men are opposed to military build-ups and war. And everything else that costs $350 billion a year.

8. Cheap men are unlikely to ask for a divorce. Not while alimony is still legal.
9. Cheap men have nice breath. From eating handfuls of after dinner mints as they walk out of restaurants.

FUNDAMENTAL PRINCIPLE
Two Cannot Live As Cheaply As One.

Good Reasons to Marry a Cheap Woman

1. Cheap women don't mind comparison shopping.
2. Cheap women are not likely to throw lavish parties.
3. Cheap women will never bounce a check or exceed the credit limit on a charge card.
4. When asked for a charitable donation, cheap women will almost automatically respond, "My husband gives at the office."
5. Cheap women will not buy exotic underwear or other ridiculous and expensive stuff.
6. A cheap woman will not want to send the kids to private school.
7. A cheap women will cheerfully save discount coupons.
8. A cheap woman will understand the wisdom of handing down clothes from one child to the next.
9. A cheap woman will never require a maid.
10. A cheap woman will not want to join a country club.

How to Avoid Taking Your Wife to a Movie
Sooner or later your wife is going to ask you to take her to a movie. By following the correct procedures you can usually

Rather than take your spouse someplace expensive,
learn to entertain her yourself at home.

avoid this costly undertaking and stay home and watch TV. Here are a few things you should do.

1. **Keep a clipping file of bad reviews.** Any time a movie is mentioned, you should be able to reel off the names of five important critics and why they think the movie stinks.
2. **Keep a file of recent muggings, rapes and murders.** When your wife mentions a movie, ask her where it's playing. Immediately relate – in gory detail – any mugging, rape or murder that has occurred in the vicinity in the last 12 months.
3. **Appeal to her romantic side.** Tell your wife you'd much rather spend the evening at home with her than with a thousand smelly strangers in a crowded theater.
4. **Once a year, take your wife to a Bergman film.** All but the most unusual people will lose their desire to see another movie for 12-15 months.
5. **If you are forced into taking your wife to a movie, there are some things you should do to insure it will never happen again:**
    a) Squirm in your seat.
    b) Point out that the critics were right.
    c) Complain to the people in front of you that you can't see over their heads.
    d) Complain to the people in back of you about anything.
    e) Spill a small coke.
    f) Point out how much more expensive popcorn is at a movie theater.
    g) If it's a comedy, don't laugh.
    h) If it's a serious movie, laugh constantly.

i) Complain about the movie all the way home and bring it up again the next morning at breakfast.

j) Above all, *make sure your wife understands that going to a movie with you will never be any fun.*

With appropriate modifications, these techniques may also be applied to nightclubs, concerts, theaters and any other cultural events.

20

A CHEAP OFF THE OLD BLOCK: THE GENERAL PRINCIPLES OF CHILD REARING

Okay, so you've decided to have kids . . . it's not smart but it's your decision. Here are some ways to keep the financial damage to a minimum.

1. **Always buy clothing, shoes, hats and athletic footwear at least two sizes too big.** Children grow much too fast. Due to this, sneakers, ice skates, shorts, hats, winter coats, shorts, pants, etc. should always be purchased at least two and preferably three sizes too large. Also, make sure a child understands that a new Easter suit will have to last a minimum of seven years.

2. **Dress your children to look several years younger than they really are.** This will enable them to buy cheap tickets for movies, buses, trains, and airplanes long after their friends are paying full price.

3. **Never buy a toy advertised on TV.** There's always something similar that's a lot cheaper.

4. **A second child never gets anything new.** Same with the third, fourth, fifth and sixth.

Properly dressed child.

5. **Things a child should know are "out of the question" from the earliest possible age:**
    a) a private school education.
    b) a Porsche for his or her 17th birthday.
    c) a junior year abroad.
6. **Beliefs to discourage.** We recommend that you tell your children that the following are either dead or never existed:
    a) Santa Claus.
    b) The Tooth Fairy.
    c) The Easter Bunny.
7. **Hobbies to encourage:**
    a) Coin collecting
    b) Collecting returnable bottles
    c) Steaming off labels for cash refunds
    d) Sending away for free samples
    e) Saving string, tin foil or waxed paper
8. **Hobbies to discourage:**
    a) Yacht racing
    b) Checking Dad's pants for change.
9. **Cultural activities.** Art, music and literature can have a powerful effect on the attitudes your child develops towards money. Here are some works your child should be exposed to from infancy:
    a) "How Much Is That Doggie In The Window"
    b) "Money, Money" by the Beatles
    c) The Price is Right (TV show)
    d) "The Moneylender and his Wife," painting by Quentin Matsys, 1514
    e) "Material Girl" by Madonna

What Are Kids Good For?

Remember, there's no such thing as child labor laws when they're your own. Here are a few things you can reasonably expect your children to do for you while you're busy housing, feeding and clothing them.

Age	Tasks
1-3	Up to age 3, kids get a free ride. Never let them forget it.
3-6	Clean floors, polish silver, wash dishes, weed garden, shine shoes.
6-9	Rake lawn, cut grass, minor plumbing repairs, light carpentry.
9-12	Shingle roof, pave driveway, build fence, rewire house.
12-15	Major electrical and plumbing repairs, small additions to house, install swimming pool, build summer home.

Remember, the child labor laws don't apply when they're your own.

Cheap Pets

When your kids start nagging for a kitty, a pony or a doggie, make these practical suggestions instead.

1. **Anything that eats flies.** For example, an iguana, turtle or frog. During the summer you won't have to feed them. During the winter, they'll either hibernate or die.

2. **Mollusks, crustaceans and bivalves.** Unlike cats and dogs, these creatures require no food, flea collars, or veterinary care. Highly prized for their quiet companionship, lobsters, clams and oysters may be consumed when the constraints of ownership become too demanding.

3. **A Moosehead.** Okay, so it'll never bring you your slippers. On the other hand, it'll never make a mess on the rug, either.

4. **An ant farm.** A perennial cheapskate favorite. After the initial expense, you can feed them for months with about 3¢ worth of sugar.

5. **Roaches.** The perfect urban pet. Requires no food, leash or special training.

6. **Baby chickens.** How could anything that goes, "Cheap, cheap," be all bad?

Helping Your Child Choose the Proper Profession

During childhood, kids inevitably fantasize about the professions they will want to enter as adults. Most of these, of course, are utterly unpractical. The responsible parent should direct the child away from these professions *as soon as possible*, or be prepared to continue financing him or her forever.

Child's Choice of Profession	Area Into Which He Should Be Directed
Actor	Crop Duster
Ballerina	Shoe salesperson
Surgeon	High Wire Aerialist
Writer	Laundromat Owner
Aerial balloonist	Contortionist
Contortionist	Auto Mechanic
Sculptor	Cocaine Dealer
Indian Chief	Real Estate Developer

Contrary to the popular belief that it's a good thing to have a child enter the medical profession, we discourage this thoroughly. For one thing, a child entering the medical field will require extraordinary amounts of support and capital and will not make a cent until well into the thirties. Furthermore, once he or she does start earning vast sums of money, the earning power will not be attributed to parents but rather to his or her own hard work and intelligence. Consequently, the child will not have the proper feeling that "everything is owed to the parents." In fact, if your child becomes a doctor, you'll be lucky if you get a call once a year.

Sheepskin, no; Cheapskin, yes

There's no need to pay up to $12,000 a year, when for $50 you can get everything you need to convince the neighbors your son or daughter is attending one of the country's most prestigious universities. Here are the items you should order from the university's store.

1. College beanie
2. Three university decals (two for your car, one for your child's)

3. A framed, labelled photo depicting the most prestigious part of the campus
4. A beer stein with university seal
5. A sweatshirt or T-shirt with the university mascot

$CHEAP TRICK #14: To be really convincing, you should fabricate a college prank – for example, something about the time your kid stole the clapper from the bell tower or went on a panty raid. Repeat this story at every opportunity.

For less than $50, you can convince the neighbors your child attends one of the nation's most prestigious colleges or universities.

21

TRICK OR CHEAP? FIVE WAYS TO HANDLE THE LITTLE MONSTERS ON HALLOWEEN

I f there's anything more annoying than tipping a doorman, it's handing out candy to the hordes of greedy, grubby, kids at Halloween. Rarely do they do more than extend an open bag and grunt, urging us to drop some morsel in. Never do they thank us. The only reason most of us don't just push the little brats backwards down the stairs is the fear of reprisal – the stolen hubcap, the broken window, the splintered mailbox. There are, however, ways of getting through this ordeal more cheaply than you might expect.

1.   **Pretend you're not home.** Turn off all the lights and don't answer the door.

2.   **Never give away candy bars, candies apples or Hershey's kisses.** Kids love this stuff. Not only will they keep returning to your house year after year until they're practically adults, but they'll also tell their friends about your place.

3.   **Give candy corn.** You buy it in bulk which makes it very inexpensive – and kids hate it, which means they're likely to cross you off their Halloween list for next year.

4.   **Give an apple.** Kids hate apples even more than candy corn – and nothing says they have to be fresh.

5.   **Hand out strange gifts.** Halloween is a perfect night to get rid of all the crap that's been cluttering up your attic and basement. Instead of candy, give kids pictures of your grandmother, irons that don't work anymore, broken hammers, etc.

22

WHAT DID THEY EVER DO FOR YOU? A WORD ABOUT YOUR PARENTS

As your parents get along in years they will start to expect gifts and various forms of support from you. Naturally you will resist. Naturally they will demand. To keep friction and expenses to a minimum, there are certain well established guidelines that should be followed.

If your parents gave you:	You give them:
1. a pup tent	an oxygen tent
2. a surfboard	a shuffleboard
3. a Walkman	a walker
4. ballet lessons	a Dr Scholls' corn remover
5. a dollhouse, dog or baseball mitt	a hearing aid or blender
6. orthodontic braces	a neck brace
7. 3 square meals a day	a subscription to Reader's Digest

Sooner or later you may have to help your parents
financially. That doesn't mean you have to be happy
about it.

23

How To Avoid Taking Your Family On Vacation

When the members of your family start talking about taking a vacation, you should immediately counter by mentioning all the horrible things that happen when you get further than half a block away from home.

Warm Climate/ Summer	Cold Climate/ Winter	Europe
Sun poisoning	Frostbite	Jack the Ripper
Dysentary	Avalanches	Bubonic Plague
Dengue fever	The Abominable Snowman	Religious pogroms
Sandy beds	Slow starvation	English food
Cannibals	Skiing accidents	French waiters
Mambo snakes	Uncontrollable skidding	The Italian telephone system
Great white sharks	The Story of Donner Pass	Germans

$CHEAP TRICK #15: Early in your married life, make it a point to take your spouse on a vacation that is absolutely miserable – your honeymoon will do nicely. Make sure your spouse understands that any future vacation will be equally unenjoyable.

FUNDAMENTAL PRINCIPLE
Never take a vacation in season.

24

Words And Phrases
The Cheap Traveller
Should Know

English
1. That's too damn much.
2. I'll give you half that.
3. You've got to be kidding.
4. Geez, this bill is ridiculous!
5. You are a criminal and a thief.
6. I would not pay you that to save my mother's life.

French
1. C'est trop beaucoup.
2. Je vous donnerai le demi.
3. Vous me blaguez!
4. Geez, cet addition est ridicule!
5. Vous etes un voleur et un criminel.
6. Je ne vous payerez pas ca a sauver la vie de ma mere.

Spanish
1. ¡Es demasiado!
2. Te doy la mitad.
3. Bromeas!
4. ¡Geez, que ridiculo!
5. ¡Eres ladrón!
6. ¡No te lo pagaría para salvar la vida de mi madre!

Whenever you get a bill, smack your head and say
"Geez, this is ridiculous."

25

THE CHEAPSKATE'S CREED: THE GOLDEN RULES

1. Always split the gas.

2. Always count your change.

3. Always ask for a doggie bag.

4. Never throw anything out that could possibly be used again.

5. Never pay anyone by the hour.

6. Never turn down anything free.

7. Never leave a hotel empty handed.

Properly exploited, a hotel can provide most of the
basic necessities of life.

26

CHEAP TALK: HOW TO MAKE A LONG DISTANCE PHONE CALL

Talk is not cheap, especially if it's long distance. Here are a few questions to ask yourself before you use the phone.

1. Is it possible to reverse the charges?

2. Is it possible to make this call from a friend's house?

3. Is the person you want to call likely to call you within the next three months?

4. Could this call result in the person on the other end sending money?

5. Am I likely to inherit money from this person?

6. Could this message be communicated just as easily by (a) letter, (b) postcard, or (c) smoke signal?

$CHEAP TRICK #16: When someone makes a call from your house, always count the number of digits as they dial to make sure it's a local call.

FUNDAMENTAL PRINCIPLE
Never make a phone call across more than one time zone.

27

CHEAPSKATES HALL OF FAME

1. **Ben "A Penny Saved is A Penny Earned" Franklin.**
   A man who had the courage to name his publication "Poor Richard's Almanac" while being one of the wealthiest men in Pennsylvania.

2. **Scrooge McDuck.**

3. **Abraham Lincoln.**
   Whose face is on the penny?

4. **John D. Rockefeller.**
   While one of the wealthiest men in the world, he still courageously refused to tip a cab driver more than a dime.

5. **Jack Benny**

6. **Polonius (from "Hamlet").**
   For his advice to son, Laertes, "neither a lender nor a borrower be."

7. **Scrooge.**
   If only he'd had the guts not to repent.

8. **Roger Corman.**
Who steadfastly refused to spend more than $200,000 to make the film "Rock 'n Roll High School" which ultimately grossed over $14,000,000.00

9. **Edmund Wilson.**
The famous critic always fought with waiters about the check. Edither Oliver recalls him saying "But we didn't eat any bread. You've added it up wrong; it's *much* less."

10. **Katharine Hepburn.**
The wealthy actress never eats in restaurants. "Can't bear to pay the prices. Can't bear to see *anybody* dumb enough to pay the prices."

11. **The Hunt Family.**
Spent billions trying to corner the silver market, but still brought their lunch to work in brown paper bags.

12. **Hetty Green.**
Despite a fortune of nearly $100 million, she lived as though penniless. When a hospital asked for payment to treat her son's infected knee, she took the boy home rather than pay for it. Subsequently, his leg had to be amputated.

13. **Frederick William I of Prussia.**
The austere father of Frederick the Great, Frederick William kept his money in kegs in the cellar. He also fed the royal family rotten cabbages rather than throw them out.

14. **Marc Chagall.**
   Figuring that his signature made them collector's items and that therefore they wouldn't be cashed, Chagall paid for everything – even small purchases such as cigarettes and toothpaste – by check.

15. **Earl Butz.**
   On occasion the former Secretary of Agriculture was seen wrapping food from Capitol Hill Club parties in napkins – to take it home.

16. **John Elwes** (British 1714-1789).
   Despite a fortune of 500,000 pounds, he wore ragged clothes and a wig he'd found in the gutter. He forbade repairs on his estates; and if a servant put out hay for a visitor's horse, he would sneak out and remove it.

28

Words To Live By

1. **The buck stops here.**

2. **Waste not, want not.**

3. **A penny saved is a penny earned.**

4. **There's no such thing as a free ride.**

5. **I can't afford it.**

6. **Give no quarter.**

7. **It's in the mail.**

FUNDAMENTAL PRINCIPLE
A penny saved is well worth the effort.

29

When The Cheaps Are Down: How To Play Poker

Gambling, of course, is extraordinary and unnatural behavior for any cheapskate. Once in a while, however, you will be dragged into a poker game by "the guys." While you would rather have your fingernails removed with pliers, you're going to have to play. Here's how.

1. **Never put in your ante.** Wait 'til someone asks. Then say you forgot.

2. **If you get three of a kind or better, bid a penny.**

3. **If someone raises you more than a nickel, drop out.**

4. **Pile your money in neat stacks and count it before and after playing each hand.** If one stack starts to get low, tell everyone the wife expects you home by 11:00.

5. **Sit out every third hand.**

6. **If it's at someone else's house, eat all the potato chips and sandwiches you can.** If it's at your house, serve crudite.

No one can possibly eat more than 10 cents worth of raw
vegetables in one evening.

7. If you lose more than $1 go home.

30

Such Cheap Sorrow: Partying

The object of a party is to have a good time. How can you expect to enjoy yourself, however, when you're shelling out as much as $50 to amuse a bunch of people you probably don't even like? May we suggest the following?

1. Make it a BYOB party. Of course.

2. Refill an expensive liquor bottle with cheap booze. Don't worry, no one will know the difference.

3. Water down everything else. They may know the difference, but who cares.

4. Make sure you drink all the liquor your guests bring before you serve any of your own. If anyone shows up with a case of beer, put it in the garage.

5. If obligated to serve food, look through the refrigerator for something that's about to go bad. Mix it with sour cream and call it clam dip.

6. Invite doctors, lawyers, investment counselors and other professionals. Then spend the evening badgering them for free advice.

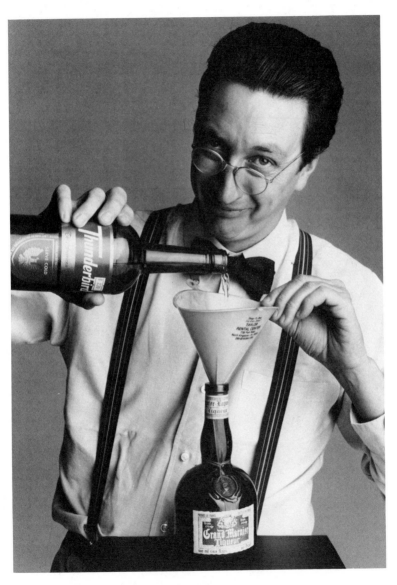

With the aid of a simple, plastic funnel, an expensive
bottle of liquor can appear to last a lifetime.

7.   Have your child dressed as a valet. Charge for parking.

FOUR RULES IF YOU'RE INVITED TO A PARTY

1.   Don't eat for three days before the party. Then stuff yourself so you won't have to eat for three days after.

2.   Get there early. With luck, you can polish off most of the hors d'oeurves before anyone else even arrives.

3.   Always bring the cheapest bottle of wine you can find.

4.   Never leave with less booze than you brought.

31
How To Handle A Request For A Loan

S ooner or later someone is going to try to borrow money from you. Here are a number of ways to handle this.

1. **The shrug and a smile.** A good technique to use with a person you don't like much, anyway. Simply shrug, smile and shake your head "no."

2. **The "Gee, I'd like to."** This technique should be used with someone who's substantially larger than you or from whom you hope to borrow money in the future. First, assure the would-be borrower that you'd like to lend him the money he wants; then give him a good excuse explaining why you can't. For instance:
    a) "Gee, I'd like to lend you $5, but I need the money for bus fare."
    b) "Gee, I'd like to lend you $10, but I promised my kid I'd take him to the movies."
    The excuse should always be emotional or of overriding immediacy. An excuse such as, "Gee, I'd like to lend you $10 but I've got to get a hammer for a birdhouse I'm going to build next year," is not convincing.

3. **The empty well.** A simple, but effective technique is to show a would-be leech that there's nary a bill in your wallet.

4. **The counter touch.** When the leech asks for money, laugh explosively and inform him that you were just about to ask him for some. A virtually fail proof method; typically he'll leave within seconds.

5. **The reminder.** As soon as the leech tries to touch you up, remind him that he owes you $10 from a loan you gave him two months ago. It is not important whether you actually loaned the person any money or not; in most cases the would-be borrower will not want to discuss the issue and can be counted on to walk away quickly.

6. **The token.** Reach in your pocket, pull out a nickel, dime or quarter and say, "That's all I've got." Typically, it's not enough.

7. **Tomorrow and tomorrow and tomorrow.** When someone asks to borrow money, ask if he can wait until tomorrow. Repeat process as often as necessary.

8. **The bleak picture.** This is the best approach to use when someone tries to borrow a lot of money. For instance, if they need it for an operation, to avoid foreclosure or to pay off a big gambling debt.
   a) When someone asks for the money, express enormous sympathy with his problem. Tell

him how much you'd like to give him the money he needs.

b) Next, tell him about your own problems. *Draw the bleakest picture possible.*

c) Break down in tears. Tell him you can really understand his dilemma, because your own problems are so overwhelming.

d) Apply the counter touch.

e) Avoid the person for the rest of your life.

Proper performance of "The Bleak Picture" may
require professional dramatic training.

32

KNOW THE ENEMY – FOR HE IS AS CHEAP AS YOU

I f you ever hope to return home with a dollar in your pocket it's important to be able to recognize fellow cheapskates. After all, the world is chockablock full of them and, let's face it, there isn't one who isn't trying to spend your money with at least as much voracity and tenacity as you expend trying to hang on to it. It is not, however, always easy to identify a fellow skinflint. The reason for this is simply that, like the vampire, a cheapskate will do almost anything to keep his true nature from being discovered; for, once identified, a cheapskate knows he will not easily be able to mooch, welch, scrounge, or skip out on his part of the bill again. Consider, for a moment, the unfortunate consequences. It means that on any given afternoon, you're likely to go to lunch with four other people at least three of whom will try and stiff you on the tab. It means that anytime you're approaching a toll booth with four other people in a car, at least three are going to pretend they don't have any change. The challenge here is to be able to differentiate those who are legitimately short of funds from those who just don't feel like coughing up an extra nickel if they can possibly avoid it. Due to the wily and deceptive public nature of the typical cheapo, this can be quite a trick. The one place in which a cheapskate almost always betrays himself, however, is home, cheap home.

So, if you want to know if someone's a closet cheapskate, just look in his closets. Also, his bedroom, living room and the kitchen sink. Here are some things you're likely to find.

1. **BURNT TOAST SCRAPINGS.** You can be sure they didn't feed the burnt toast to the dog, either.

2. **A VAST COLLECTION OF TUPPERWARE.** Come on now, who else but a real tightwad cares if half a serving of potatoes au gratin goes bad?

3. **A WEIRD SELECTION OF ASHTRAYS.** Stolen from every hotel in the western hemisphere.

4. **MOTEL SOAP, TOWELS AND BATH MATS.** Hey, you can't always stay at a hotel.

5. **A PROMOTIONAL SIZE TUBE OF TOOTHPASTE.** Squeezed flat. Probably taken from the same motel as the soap.

6. **ENOUGH TOILET PAPER TO LAST TWO AVERAGE FAMILIES A LIFETIME.** But, it was on sale.

7. **A FILE OF DISCOUNT COUPONS.** Alphabetized and kept up to date.

8. **PLASTIC COUCH COVERS.** Made from plastic thick enough to withstand a direct nuclear attack. In this household, there is no intention of buying another couch. Ever.

9. **FOURTEEN YEAR OLD UNDERWEAR.** So what if the elastic hasn't snapped since the Bicentennial year? So what if it has more holes than a championship golf course? Who's going to see it anyway?

33

THESE ARE A FEW OF OUR FAVORITE THINGS

1. Happy Hour
2. Free hors d'oeuvres
3. Finding a coin in the sand
4. All-you-can-eat restaurants
5. Money back guarantees
6. "No tipping" signs
7. Finding a parking meter with time left on it.
8. Winning free games on a pinball machine
9. A "Dutch" date
10. Garage sales
11. Reduced price matinees
12. Piggy banks
13. One cent sales.

FUNDAMENTAL PRINCIPLE
There's no such thing as getting your money's worth.

34

How To Dress

Many of the wealthiest men in the world dress like bums, and there is a method to their madness. For if you dress expensively, you will invariably be billed accordingly. Thus, whenever possible, and *on every occasion in which you're dealing with a tradesman*, make sure you look as poor as possible. Wear a flannel shirt with strong armpit odor, stained pants and beat-up shoes. When negotiating with a gardener this can save you as much as $25 a week. When getting an estimate on body work for your car, it can save $300 on a simple dented fender.

In a situation in which you must wear a suit, make sure it is at least ten years old and/or looks like it once belonged to the Polish ambassador. This manner of dress is indispensable any time you're dealing with the IRS, involved in business negotiations or dealing with an in-law who wants a loan.

FUNDAMENTAL PRINCIPLE
Remember, if you're dressed expensively, they'll know you have money. If you're not, they can never be sure.

35

The Corporate Cheapskate

Running a company gives the true cheapskate a chance to practice his art on a whole different level. Here are a few of the practices every corporate cheapo should be familiar with.

1. Charge your employees for coffee. Cream and sugar are extra, of course.

2. Give 'em a title instead of a raise. So what do you care if the janitor is a vice-president?

3. Leave the office when somebody announces a wedding or has an important birthday. If you're there, you'll probably have to contribute to a gift. As if it isn't bad enough that you have to give them a watch when they retire!

4. Eliminate the water cooler. If you have to have one, put it outside your office door, where you can keep an eye on it.

36

SWING LOW, CHEAP CHARIOT

While, of course, a cheapskate can be expected to enjoy dying no more than anyone else, he can at least take solace in a few comforting thoughts.

1. In all likelihood, you won't have to pay for your own funeral.

2. You'll never have to tip a doorman again.

3. Vacations will be much less expensive.

4. You'll never have to buy new clothes.

5. You'll never have to pay taxes.

6. You'll never be asked to contribute to another charity.

37

WASTE NOT, WANT NOT

Recycling isn't just for tin cans and glass bottles anymore. With the least bit of rinsing and ironing, here are a few of the things you should be able to use ad infinitum.

1. Saran Wrap

2. Dental floss

3. Aluminum foil

4. Q-tips

5. Paper towels

With a little thought, you could easily expand this list to include at least two or three more handy household items.

With proper maintenance, a single sheet of aluminum foil can last indefinitely.

38

THIRTY DAYS TO A CHEAPER YOU

Now that you've learned the lessons, it is time to put them into practice. Whether you're a naturally magnanimous person who wants to develop a new, cheap attitude or an accomplished cheapo who wants to brush up a little, you'll find this regimen invaluable.

DAY 1: Go to a bar for Happy Hour. Leave as soon as drinks are full price.

DAY 2: Take a magazine out of the library. Cut out all the coupons and return it.

DAY 3: Go to a flea market and haggle with a merchant. After you get him down as low as possible, decide you don't want to buy the item after all.

DAY 4: Go to a food store that's giving away free samples of cheese. Hang around until you've eaten all of them.

DAY 5: Go to lunch with a friend. Underpay your portion of the bill by at least $2.00.

DAY 6: Look for pennies on the street. When you find one go to a 1¢ sale.

DAY 7: Borrow a cup of liquid laundry detergent from a neighbor. While you're there, see what else you can get – fabric softener, Static Guard, etc.

DAY 8: Go to a special low price movie matinee . . . pay no more than $1.50.

DAY 9: Go shopping at a Salvation Army store.

DAY 10: Offer a co-worker a ride to work. Charge him 22¢ a mile.

DAY 11: Go comparison shopping in at least four supermarkets. Don't buy anything 'til you're sure you have the lowest price.

DAY 12: Decide not to buy a new car for at least another year.

DAY 13: Go out for pizza with friends. Eat as many pieces as you can as fast as you can.

DAY 14: Spend the afternoon looking for forgotten coins in vending machines.

DAY 15: Go to a free theatrical production at the local high school. If they "pass the hat" contribute a quarter.

DAY 16 (Summer): Buy a Coke and sit in a restaurant all afternoon to take advantage of the free air conditioning.

DAY 16 (Winter): Turn your heat down to 55°. Visit with friends until it's time to go to bed.

DAY 17: Go to a neighborhood tavern and nurse a beer while you watch their wide screen TV.

DAY 18: Wash off a piece of previously used Saran Wrap, let it dry and use it again.

DAY 19: Stop at a garage sale, ask the price of everything and don't buy anything.

DAY 20: When someone comes to the door to ask for a charitable contribution, pretend you're not home.

DAY 21: Go window shopping.

DAY 22: Go through your neighborhood collecting used plastic margarine tubs. Clean and save for future use.

DAY 23: Send away for a product that gives you two weeks to try it free. After two weeks, send it back.

DAY 24: Re-use a piece of aluminum foil.

With the use of a properly marked training glass, you can easily learn to nurse a single glass of beer up to 2½ hours.

DAY 25: Refuse to give your children a raise in allowance.

DAY 26: Subscribe to MONEY magazine.

DAY 27: Return a half eaten wedge of cheese (1 lb. or more) for a full refund.

DAY 28: Buy a cheap ticket to a concert or a show. As soon as the house lights go down, sneak up to the expensive seats.

DAY 29: Go to the Post Office and mail something manuscript rate when you should have paid first class.

DAY 30: Take the family out to dinner. Ask for separate checks.

A POSTSCRIPT

I n exploring the ways you can scrimp and save and get by for less, I'm afraid I've only scratched the surface. Cheapness is such a wonderfully unlimited topic that it would require a set of volumes far greater than the Encylopedia Brittanica to cover it thoroughly.

Thus, the best thing I can do is *not* try and point out every little thing you can do to save a buck, but rather to encourage you to use your own energy and imagination and bring a full sense of your own frugal potential to your daily activities *each and every day of your life*! Given a little courage and a dash of cunning, there is no end to the ways you can get more and pay less. Above all, I hope I've been able to instill a sense of pride in your cheapness that has long been denied us.

In closing, go forth and multiply. Also divide, add and subtract. And above all, make sure you get your money's worth.